SPOTLIGHT ON EXPLORERS AND COLONIZATION™

CHRISTOPHER COLUMBUS

Explorer and Colonizer of the New World

HENRIETTA TOTH

ROSEN PUBLISHING®
New York

For my niece Emi, who likes to explore new places

Published in 2017 by The Rosen Publishing Group, Inc.
29 East 21st Street, New York, NY 10010

Copyright © 2017 by The Rosen Publishing Group, Inc.

First Edition

Library of Congress Cataloging-in-Publication Data

Names: Toth, Henrietta, author.
Title: Christopher Columbus : explorer and colonizer of the New World / Henrietta Toth.
Description: First edition. | New York : Rosen Publishing, 2017. | Series: Spotlight on explorers and colonization | Includes bibliographical references and index. | Audience: Grades 5-10.
Identifiers: LCCN 2016003839| ISBN 9781477787984 (library bound) | ISBN 9781477787977 (pbk.) | ISBN 9781499438024 (6-pack)
Subjects: LCSH: Columbus, Christopher. | Explorers--America--Biography. | Explorers--Spain--Biography. | America--Discovery and exploration--Spanish.
Classification: LCC E111 .T68 2016 | DDC 970.01/5092--dc23
LC record available at http://lccn.loc.gov/2016003839

Manufactured in the United States of America

CONTENTS

THE COLUMBUS WE KNOW

Most people know Christopher Columbus as the explorer who discovered America in 1492. At least that is what was believed and taught for a long time. Students even learned a poem about Columbus. The first line is, "In 1492, Columbus sailed the ocean blue."

But was Columbus really the first navigator to reach the shores of the New World? There is evidence that other explorers might have traveled to the North American continent as many as five hundred years before Columbus.

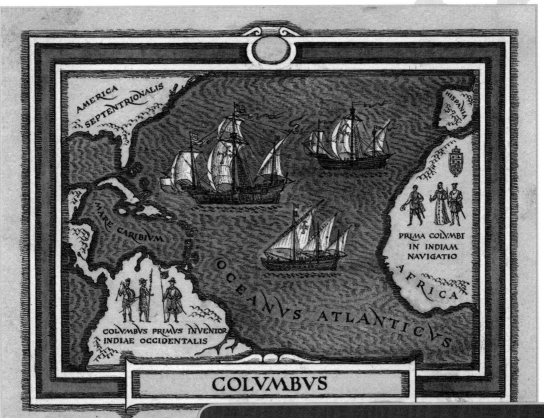

Christopher Columbus's first voyage to the Americas is depicted in this 2003 watercolor and ink map by Russian artist Yaroslav Gerzhedovich.

If Columbus was not the first person to discover the New World, how did he become a key figure in American history? Columbus is important for three reasons. One, he did discover and explore new lands. Two, Columbus started an ocean passage between Europe and the Americas. Three, and perhaps most important, Columbus's explorations marked the modern colonization of the New World.

THE TRUTH ABOUT COLUMBUS

If Columbus was not the first explorer to discover the Americas, then what is the truth about him? Some scholars think Columbus is overrated in the history of America. It is true that he was seeking a westward ocean route to the Indies, which he never found. This search led him to the Americas instead, but he always believed that he had landed in Asia. Columbus never set foot on the North American mainland.

Columbus was also in search of gold and other riches such as silver, pearls, and spices. His actions were sometimes clouded by his ambitions for fame and belief in his own importance. He was cruel to the natives

Leif Eriksson points to the North American continent from his longboat, as imagined in this oil painting by Norwegian artist Christian Krohg.

he encountered in the Americas and even to the crews of his ships.

If Columbus did not discover America, then who did? The Viking explorer Leif Eriksson is believed to have reached the North American continent in 1000, nearly five hundred years before Columbus. Legends also claim that Irish monks sailed across the North Sea to present-day Newfoundland even before Leif Eriksson. There is also evidence that English and Portuguese fishing boats might have sailed as far as Newfoundland almost two hundred years before Columbus traveled another route across the Atlantic.

COLUMBUS'S CHILDHOOD

Christopher Columbus was born in the town of Genoa in present-day Italy. In Italian, Columbus's name was Cristoforo Colombo. He was born in 1451, probably in October. Columbus had four brothers and one sister. His father was a weaver of wool, and his mother's family were also weavers. Columbus did not have much formal schooling. He helped his father in the family's weaving business, and it was probably expected that he would learn the weaving trade.

Genoa was a busy seaport on the Mediterranean Sea. Ships and their crews traveled in and out of port loading and unloading all sorts of goods. Columbus found

A group of weavers work at their trade making tapestries and cloth. This is a section from a mural painted about 1470 on a wall in a palace in northern Italy.

seafaring more exciting than weaving, and at about the age of fourteen he went to sea. He worked as a cabin boy doing many different chores, including cleaning and cooking. Columbus took several short fishing trips and also traveled as far as Ireland and Iceland.

COLUMBUS'S EARLY ADULTHOOD

As a young adult Columbus was determined that a life at sea would be his career. He wanted to be a sea captain, and he wanted to be famous and wealthy. Columbus's early work aboard ships taught him some skills—like steering a ship—on which he started to build his future.

Columbus was largely self-educated. He read about natural history, astronomy, navigation, and mathematics. He also learned to speak Portuguese, Spanish, and Latin. He was described as being confident and determined, which are good qualities for a

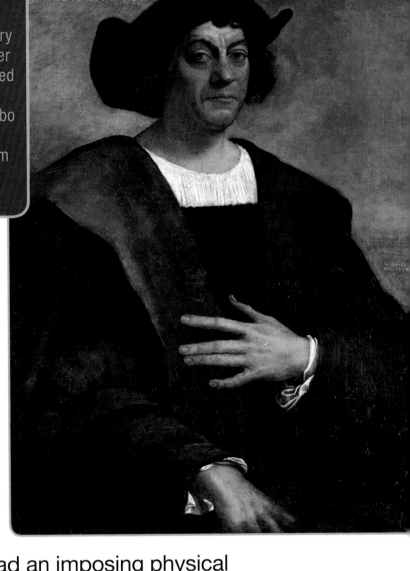

navigator. Yet he was also known to be stubborn, bad-tempered, and arrogant.

Columbus had an imposing physical appearance. No portraits from his lifetime exist, but he was described as being tall with a strong build. He had blue eyes and a blond beard and hair that turned white in early adulthood. The Italian artist Titian may have painted a portrait of Columbus, but there is not enough evidence to prove it.

LIFE BEFORE THE VOYAGES

Before Columbus made his four major expeditions across the Atlantic Ocean, he sailed on short merchant voyages. In 1476 he was in a shipwreck near Portugal. He survived and made his way to Lisbon, the capital of Portugal. Columbus lived there for several years running a mapmaking business with his brother, Bartolomeo. He married Doña Felipa and had a son, Diego.

Columbus created maps for sea captains and merchants who talked of finding an ocean route to the Indies. A route on water would be more direct than traveling thousands of miles over land through several countries that sometimes were dangerous. Plus, whoever found this new way to the

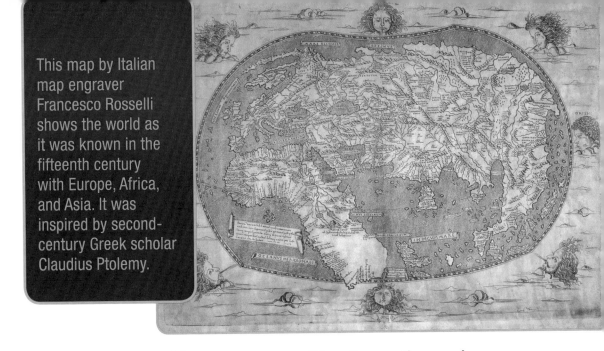

Indies would become wealthy from the spice trade. Columbus believed that he could find the new route. He studied the travels of explorer and merchant Marco Polo, who took the Silk Road to Asia in the late thirteenth century.

In 1484 Columbus asked King John II of Portugal to fund his westward trip to the Indies, but the king was not convinced by Columbus's plans. Columbus moved to the city of Córdoba in Spain. In 1491 he successfully petitioned King Ferdinand and Queen Isabella of Spain to fund his voyage. He also demanded to have the title of "Admiral of the Ocean Sea" and to rule any lands he might discover.

COLUMBUS AS MARITIME NAVIGATOR

In Columbus's time, it was thought that there was one large body of water that surrounded the continents of Europe, Asia, and Africa. It was called the Ocean Sea. Other navigators had tried to reach the Indies by sailing around the tip of Africa and then going east, but the trip was too difficult and they turned back. Columbus was convinced that he could find the westward route across the Ocean Sea. Many people thought his plan was foolhardy.

Columbus was not the most experienced navigator, and he miscalculated the earth's diameter as being smaller. Like most captains and sailors of his time, Columbus sailed by dead reckoning. Using maps and charts, he measured the distances and set his course for certain routes by using a compass. He may have followed a map made by Henricus Martellus, which showed Europe, Africa, and Asia but not the Americas. Columbus navigated the ocean by watching the sun, stars, moon, and curve of the earth, but he was not very good at it. He also followed the trade winds and the currents. He believed that God was his co-navigator and meant for him to find the westward route to the Indies.

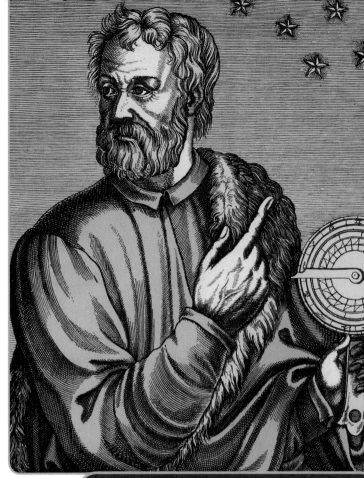

Columbus holds an astrolabe in this late fifteenth-century engraving. Astrolabes helped navigators determine time based on the positions of the sun, moon, stars, and planets.

THE FIRST VOYAGE, 1492

On August 3, 1492, Christopher Columbus began his voyage in search of a westward ocean route to the Indies. Columbus and his crew of nearly ninety men set sail from Palos, Spain, aboard three ships. Two brothers, Vincente Pinzón and Martin Pinzón, were captains of the caravels *Niña* and *Pinta*, which were small but fast boats. Columbus was captain of the sixty-foot (eighteen-meter) cargo ship *Santa María*. He was also commander of the fleet and voyage. The ships were loaded with food and other supplies for what could be a long trip.

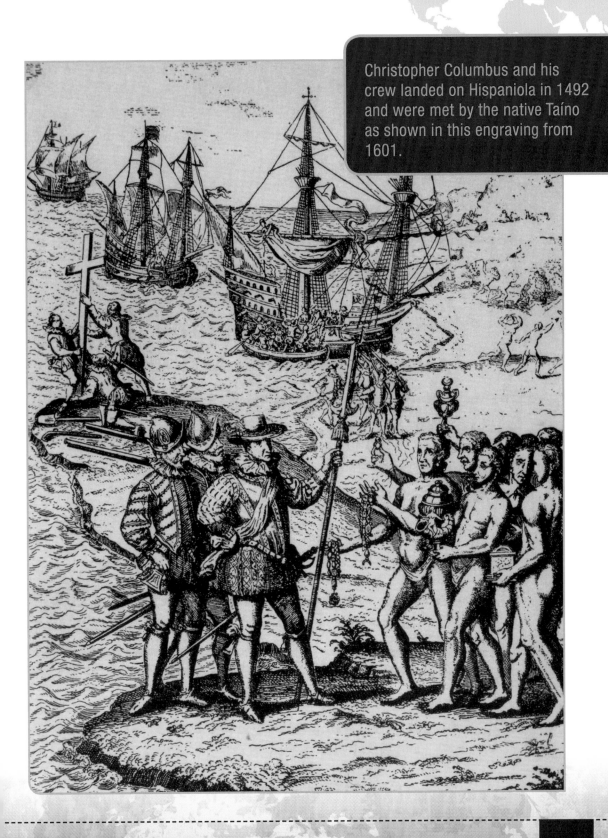

Christopher Columbus and his crew landed on Hispaniola in 1492 and were met by the native Taíno as shown in this engraving from 1601.

Columbus sailed his fleet south to the Canary Islands off the coast of Africa and then across the Atlantic Ocean. The crew did not see land for several weeks. This seemed an unusually long time to the sailors. Finally, they made landfall on October 12, 1492. Columbus believed that he had reached Japan in the Indies. Instead, he had found a New World by landing on the island of San Salvador in present-day Bahamas.

This is the archaeological site in present-day Haiti where Columbus is believed to have set up his colony, La Navidad.

San Salvador was tropical with unusual plants and birds. It was also home to native people called Taíno. They had never seen Europeans and were curious about Columbus, his crew, and his ships. Columbus did not find any riches on San Salvador, so he sailed south. He kidnapped some Taíno to help him communicate with native people on other islands. Columbus landed in Cuba and then Hispaniola—an island now comprised of two nations, Haiti and the Dominican Republic. Still, there were no great riches to be found.

On December 15, 1492, the *Santa María* hit a reef and sank off the coast of Hispaniola. Without the *Santa María*, not all the men could return home. Columbus ordered a fort to be built and called it La Navidad. Nearly forty men stayed behind to explore and search for gold until Columbus could return for them. Columbus then sailed home aboard the *Niña* along with the *Pinta*. He took some gold and native plants and birds and was welcomed in Spain as a hero.

THE SECOND VOYAGE, 1493

On September 25, 1493, Columbus set sail on his second ocean voyage. He was to bring back the crew left behind at La Navidad, the fort on Hispaniola. This time Columbus knew the route, but he still believed that he was heading west to the Indies. He did not know that he had found a New World.

Columbus commanded a larger fleet of seventeen ships and more than twelve hundred men. There were fifteen caravels, including the *Niña*, and two cargo ships. One cargo ship was named *Santa María* for the one that sank off the coast of Hispaniola.

Columbus's fleet sailed southwest from Spain and arrived in the Caribbean Islands.

The crew explored several islands, including Dominica, Guadeloupe, the Virgin Islands, and Puerto Rico. The land was lush and green, but the native Caribs were not welcoming. Columbus and his crew then arrived on November 27, 1493, at La Navidad, the fort they had built during the first voyage. They found the fort burned out and learned from the Taíno that some men had fought with each other and that others had been killed in a dispute with the native people.

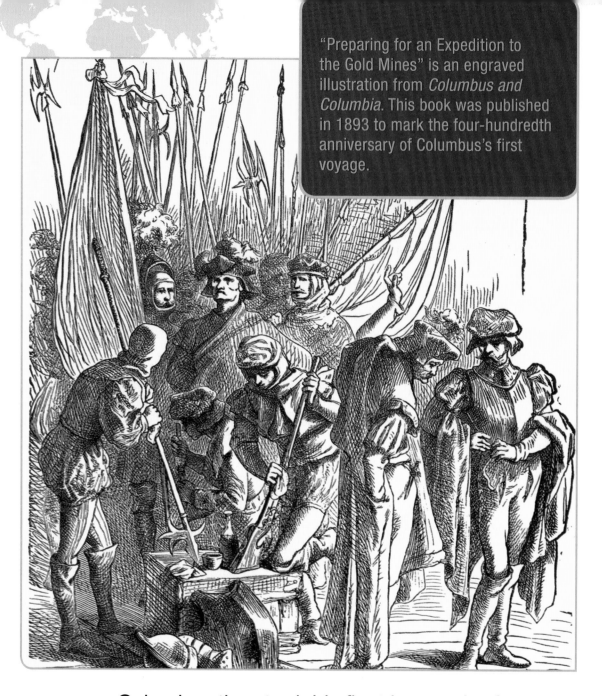

Columbus then took his fleet in search of land for a new settlement. They found it on the northern coast of Hispaniola, but it soon proved to be swampy and bug infested, making many of the men sick. The new settlement was named La Isabela for Queen Isabella of Spain. As the first Spanish colony in the New World, it would struggle to survive until abandoned only a few years later.

Columbus was governor of this new colony, but he ruled in a greedy and unfair manner, which angered the colonists. He treated the natives as slaves and forced them to mine for gold. He kept most of the little gold that was found. He left Hispaniola for a few weeks to search for mainland China but returned having found only Cuba and Jamaica.

On March 10, 1496, Columbus and some of his crew returned to Spain for supplies for the new colony. They had found very little gold, but Columbus took several hundred natives back as slaves. He had tried to convert the natives to Christianity, but they fought against European control. When Columbus reached Spain in July of 1496, Queen Isabella was not pleased that he had brought slaves with him. She considered them Spanish subjects and ordered that they be returned to their native home.

THE THIRD VOYAGE, 1498

On his two earlier voyages, Columbus had found several new islands. However, he had not found the main continent of the Indies, which he believed was near these islands. Despite Columbus's lack of success and difficulties on the earlier explorations, King Ferdinand and Queen Isabella of Spain approved a third voyage. Columbus was to take supplies for the colony of La Isabela on Hispaniola and continue his search for the westward route to the Indies.

Columbus organized a fleet of six ships that sailed from Spain on May 30, 1498. Three ships went directly to the New World with supplies. Columbus led the other three ships south of the islands he had already discovered in hopes of finding the Asian continent.

A page from the sixteenth-century Livro das Armadas manuscript describes the men and ships' captains who sailed with Columbus on his third voyage in 1498.

With little wind to push the sails, the trip took longer than before. Finally, on August 1, 1498, the crew made landfall on the island of Trinidad. From there the three ships sailed on, reaching the coast of the South American continent in present-day Venezuela. Columbus thought he had now found a new continent that was part of China.

Next, Columbus returned to Hispaniola to rule as governor. He found the colonists and natives in a violent protest against Columbus's brothers, who had been left in charge. Columbus also managed the colony in a cruel way. Spain sent a new governor to replace him, and he was arrested for governing like a tyrant. He was sent to prison and then returned to Spain in chains. After several more weeks in jail, King Ferdinand cleared Columbus of blame. However, the king took away all of Columbus's titles, including "Admiral of the Ocean Sea."

In 1498 another explorer reached the Indies by an ocean route. Vasco da Gama

Columbus is arrested in Hispaniola in 1500 by Spanish soldier Francisco de Bobadilla. This illustration is from the *General History of the Indies*, written between 1527 and 1561.

sailed around the tip of Africa, arriving in India on May 20. After trading with the people of India, da Gama returned to Portugal a hero.

THE FOURTH VOYAGE, 1502

Columbus was weary from his earlier expeditions. Yet he again convinced the king and queen of Spain to fund one more voyage. This time Columbus hoped to find a westward route to the Indian Ocean that would take him to the Indies. The Spanish monarchs agreed because explorer Vasco da Gama was already on another voyage. Da Gama could bring back untold riches for Portugal, and Spain wanted riches, too. However, the king and queen forbid Columbus from landing on Hispaniola and from taking natives as slaves.

Columbus started his final voyage on May 9, 1502. He had a small fleet of four ships and about 135 men. The crew sailed along

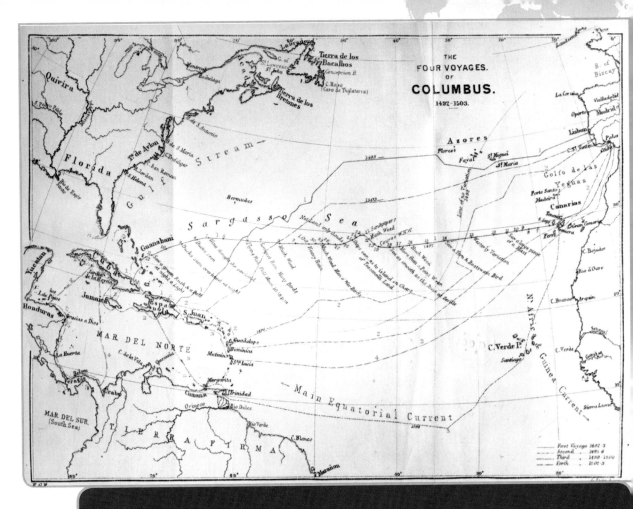

This map traces the routes that Christopher Columbus traveled on his four voyages. It appeared in *The World's Great Explorers* by J. Scott Keltic, published in 1889.

the Moroccan coast of northern Africa and then on to the Caribbean and Central America. The fourth voyage was the fastest of Columbus's trips. Strong trade winds pushed the fleet across the Atlantic Ocean in twenty-one days.

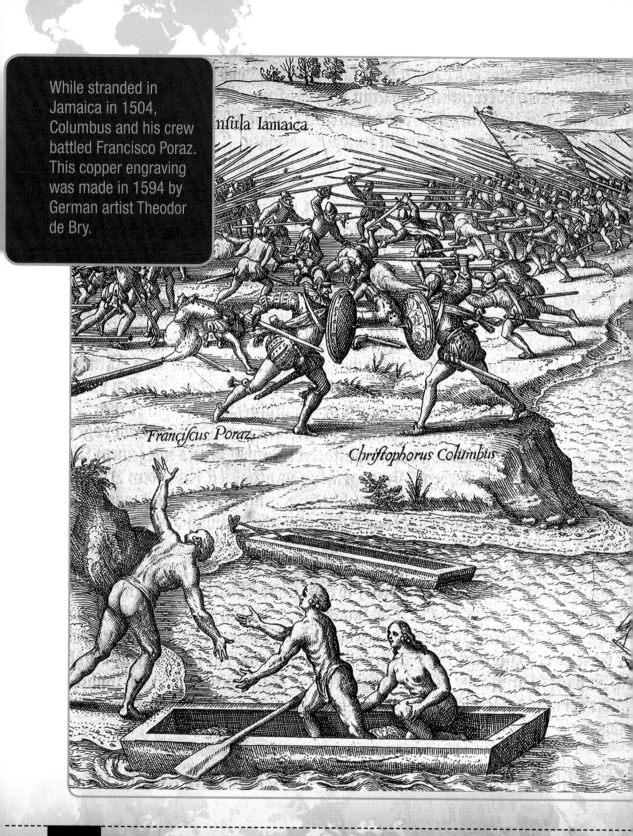

While stranded in Jamaica in 1504, Columbus and his crew battled Francisco Poraz. This copper engraving was made in 1594 by German artist Theodor de Bry.

Infula Iamaica.

Franciscus Poraz.

Chriftophorus Columbus

However, this voyage was also the most dangerous. As Columbus sailed near the Caribbean, a hurricane was forming. Columbus asked the governor of Hispaniola to allow his crew to land there, but he refused. Columbus tried to sail his ships away from the storm and anchored them in a cove for shelter. On the night of June 30, 1502, the hurricane battered the ships and pushed them out to sea.

Columbus searched on for gold and found some in present-day Panama, where he built a fort. At first the native people were friendly. Then they became hostile and attacked Columbus and his men, causing them to abandon the fort. The crew fled to the coast of Jamaica, where they were stranded for a year. Columbus sent two men to Hispaniola to buy a stronger ship to sail home to Spain.

Columbus arrived in Spain on November 7, 1504. He never found the ocean route to the Indies or the great riches that he wanted.

LIFE AFTER THE VOYAGES

Columbus returned to Spain from his fourth and last voyage in November 1504. He was in poor health, with his eyesight and mind failing. A few weeks after Columbus returned, Queen Isabella of Spain died. She had been his biggest supporter for the voyages. Columbus thought he deserved more reward for his explorations. He continued to ask King Ferdinand of Spain for recognition and money.

Columbus became ill and bedridden. Modern scholars now think that Columbus had a disease that causes inflammation throughout the body.

On May 20, 1506, Columbus died of heart failure in Valladolid, Spain. Until his death, he remained convinced that he had found parts of Asia and a new route to the Indies. He did not know that he had in fact explored new islands in the Americas.

Columbus was buried first in Spain. His remains were then moved to Hispaniola in the New World, where he had wished to be buried. Later, his bones were thought to have been returned to Spain. Scholars are still not certain where Columbus is buried.

The tomb of Christopher Columbus stands just inside the doors of Seville Cathedral in Seville, Spain.

WRITINGS BY COLUMBUS

Columbus had little formal education during his childhood. As an adult, he read and studied several subjects. This self-education probably helped Columbus write his ships' logbooks, journals of his voyages, and letters. He wrote mostly in Spanish, but there is evidence that he might also have been able to write in Italian. Hundreds of diaries, documents, and letters that Columbus wrote survive today. Some of his letters are on display at the Galata Museum of the Sea in Genoa, Italy.

Columbus kept logbooks with details about his voyages. He wrote about how the ships were navigated and the crew's experiences on the newly discovered islands. He described the "health-giving rivers and beautiful mountains" on Hispaniola.

When Columbus returned from his first voyage on March 15, 1493, he wrote a letter to King Ferdinand and Queen Isabella of Spain. He reported his discoveries of these new lands: "I discovered many islands inhabited by numerous people. I took possession of all of them for our most fortunate King." Columbus called the native Taíno "fearful and timid" people who "might become Christians and inclined to love our King and Queen ... of Spain."

Christopher Columbus wrote this letter to the Genovese ambassador to the Spanish court. It is dated March 21, 1502.

COLUMBUS'S LEGACY

Christopher Columbus did not land on the North American continent, and he did not discover America. He tried four times to reach the Indies by a westward ocean route. He died believing that he had found undiscovered islands in the Indies, even though he did not reach the Asian continent. Although none of his trips were successful in reaching the Indies, the voyages were still important.

Columbus was the first Christian European known to have landed in the Americas and discovered these new lands. He also began the exploration and colonization of the New World. However, this brought disease, death, and environmental and social changes to the

native people.

Columbus did prove that transatlantic ocean travel was possible. He showed that trade winds and currents could carry ships across the sea with more certainty than was once thought.

PLACE NAMES, STATUES, AND STAMPS

Christopher Columbus has been honored with statues, monuments, postage stamps, and places and streets named for him. Cities in Ohio, Georgia, Indiana, Mississippi, and Nebraska bear his name. There is a Christopher Columbus Boulevard in Philadelphia, Pennsylvania. A traffic circle in midtown Manhattan with a statue of the explorer is called Columbus Circle.

Hundreds of statues of Columbus have been erected in cities worldwide, from Washington, DC, to Genoa in Italy and Madrid in Spain. Many monuments to Columbus were installed in 1892 to commemorate the four-hundredth anniversary of his first voyage

MONTSERRAT

EIIR

Discovery by Columbus
1493

35
CENTS

COLUMBUS SIGHTING MONTSERRAT

in 1492. A copy statue of Columbus sits on the Capitol Square of the city named for him in Columbus, Ohio. In New York City, a bronze statue of Columbus is in Central Park.

Montserrat issued this stamp in 1973 to mark the 480th anniversary of Christopher Columbus sighting and naming the Caribbean island.

However, not everyone agrees that Columbus should be recognized. In October 2015, the Columbus statue in front of City Hall in Detroit, Michigan, was vandalized.

Columbus has also appeared on commemorative stamps. In 1893 a set of sixteen US stamps was printed showing scenes from Columbus's voyages. A sheet of forty Columbus stamps was issued in 1992.

CELEBRATING COLUMBUS

If Christopher Columbus did not truly discover America, then why do Americans celebrate Columbus Day? The holiday honors the explorer's accomplishment of landing in the New World. Columbus Day has also come to celebrate the heritage of Italian Americans, immigration to America, and this country's cultural diversity. Columbus Day is marked in many towns with fairs and parades. The largest parade is held in New York City.

Columbus Day was first observed in the eighteenth century. In 1937 it was declared a national holiday by President Franklin D. Roosevelt. Since 1970 the holiday has been observed on the second Monday in October.

Representing the ships that Christopher Columbus sailed to the New World, this float makes its way down Fifth Avenue in New York City during the Columbus Day Parade.

Columbus Day is also celebrated in other countries in the Americas and in Italy and Spain.

In the nineteenth century, people who associated Columbus Day with immigration and Catholicism did not want the holiday celebrated. In recent years, Native Americans have protested that Columbus Day celebrates not a hero but a man who brought destruction to native people. In South Dakota, Columbus Day is now observed as Native American Day.

GLOSSARY

caravel A small and fast ship used on long voyages in the fifteenth and sixteenth centuries by the Portuguese and Spanish.

colonize To form a new settlement that has ties to a parent country.

commemorate To honor someone or something with a statue, stamp, or event.

compass An instrument used to find directions.

continent A large landmass.

expedition A journey taken usually for the purpose of exploration.

fleet A large and organized group of ships.

Indies The name for a group of countries that includes Asia and India.

landfall Arriving on land by ship or plane.

legacy Something that is handed down from the past.

legends Stories told over time that become accepted as truth.

logbook A book in which details of a trip are recorded.

mainland The main mass of land of a country.

merchant Someone who buys and sells goods for a profit.

native Belonging to a place by birth.

navigate To move a ship through water.

seafaring To journey by sea.

trade The business of buying and selling goods.

trade winds Winds that blow in a constant direction to the east.

Columbus Citizens Foundation
8 East 69th Street
New York, NY 10021
(212) 249-9923
Website: http://www.columbuscitizensfd.org
This organization recognizes Italian American heritage
and organizes the New York City Columbus Day
Parade, which celebrates the historic voyages of
Christopher Columbus.

The Columbus Foundation
British Virgin Islands
(787) 672-2152
Website: http://www.thenina.com/index.html
Tours are offered of these replicas of two of Columbus's
ships, the *Niña* and the *Pinta*. Caravels such as
these were commonly sailed in Columbus's time.

Florida Museum of Natural History
University of Florida Cultural Plaza
3215 Hull Road
Gainesville, FL 32611
(352) 392-1721
Website: http://www.flmnh.ufl.edu
The museum's archaeology program and collections
cover the time during which Columbus traveled to
the New World.

Santa María Kiosk
Marina do Funchal
Funchal-Madeira 9000-055
(351) 291-220-327
Website: http://www.madeirapirateboat.com
A replica of Columbus's flagship, the *Santa María*, is
 on Madeira, an island that is an autonomous region
 of Portugal. Three-hour sailing tours aboard this
 ship offer a sense of what Columbus's voyages
 might have been like.

Websites

Because of the changing nature of Internet links,
Rosen Publishing has developed an online list of
websites related to the subject of this book. This site
is updated regularly. Please use this link to access
this list:

http://www.rosenlinks.com/SEC/chris

Allen, Kathy. *When Did Columbus Arrive in the Americas?: And Other Questions About Columbus's Voyages.* New York, NY: Lerner Publishing Group, 2012.

Bader, Bonnie. *Who Was Christopher Columbus?* New York, NY: Grosset & Dunlap, 2013.

Carlson Berne, Emma. *Did Christopher Columbus Really Discover America?: And Other Questions About the New World.* New York, NY: Sterling Children's Books, 2015.

Columbus, Christopher. *The Log of Christopher Columbus's First Voyage to America in the Year 1492.* Eastford, CT: Martino Publishing, 2011.

Gunderson, Jessica. *Christopher Columbus: New World Explorer or Fortune Hunter?* North Mankato, MN: Capstone Press, 2013.

Higgins, Nadia. *Columbus and the Journey to the New World.* Vero Beach, FL: Rourke Educational Media, 2014.

Hunter, Nick. *Christopher Columbus and Neil Armstrong: Comparing People From the Past.* Portsmouth, NH: Heinemann Publishing, 2015.

Loewen, James W. *Lies My Teacher Told Me About Christopher Columbus: What Your History Books Got Wrong.* New York, NY: New Press, 2014.

Reis, Ronald A. *Christopher Columbus and the Age of Exploration for Kids: With 21 Activities.* Chicago, IL: Chicago Review Press, 2013.

BIBLIOGRAPHY

Appelbaum, Yoni. "How Columbus Day Fell Victim to Its Own Success." *Atlantic*, October 8, 2012 (http://www.theatlantic.com).

Griffiths, Sarah. "Columbus' Map Reveals More Secrets: Scans Uncover New Locations and Written Passages on Martellus Atlas." *Daily Mail*, June 12, 2015 (http://www.dailymail.co.uk).

Heather, James. "Columbus Day: What Illness Did Christopher Columbus Battle?" Medical Daily, October 9, 2011 (http://www.medicaldaily.com).

Klein, Christopher. "10 Things You May Not Know About Christopher Columbus." History, A&E Television Network, October 5, 2012 (http://www.history.com).

Luzer, Daniel. "How We Discovered That Christopher Columbus Didn't Get to America First." *Pacific Standard Magazine*, October 14, 2013 (http://www.psmag.com).

Mariners' Museum: Exploration Through the Ages. "Christopher Columbus." Retrieved October 28, 2015 (http://ageofex.marinersmuseum.org/).

Medieval Sourcebook. "Christopher Columbus: Extracts from Journal." March 1996 (http://legacy.fordham.edu/halsall/source/columbus1.asp).

Morgan, Edmund S. "Columbus' Confusion About the New World." *Smithsonian Magazine*, October 2009 (http://www.smithsonianmag.com).

INDEX

About the Author

Henrietta Toth is a writer and editor with nearly twenty years' experience in academic publishing. She enjoys reading and writing about early world history as a career as well as a hobby.

Photo Credits

Designer: Nicole Russo; Editor: Meredith Day; Photo Researcher: Sherri Jackson